Girl Friend

& Other Mysteries of Love

• New and Selected Poems •

Charles P. Ries

Propaganda Press

Publishing division of Alternating Current Arts Co-op

Palo Alto, California

Girl Friend & Other Mysteries of Love
Charles P. Ries
©2013 Charles P. Ries, Propaganda Press

Design and Editor: Leah Angstman
leahangstman.blogspot.com

Propaganda Press
Publishing division of Alternating Current Arts Co-op
Palo Alto, California

For the most current contact and ordering information, visit:
alternatingcurrentarts.blogspot.com

Library of Congress Control Number:
ISBN 978-0615764344
First Edition: February 2013

God bless the small press

Girl Friend
& Other Mysteries of Love

Table of Contents

Contents

Girl Friend

& Other Mysteries of Love

for Joan

Blessing, Friend, Lover

I Love

Your grilled cheese sandwiches under
the full March moon, as Jupiter draws
near and we witness its unblinking eye
hovering above the horizon at early dusk.

The way your lip is slightly twisted upward
at one corner, making your mouth look like
an irregular right triangle.

Your explanation for washing your bed
sheets three times a week: "dust mites."

Your mantric complaint about how hard it is
to dress well at 20 below zero in the midst of
a blizzard. Yet refusing to compromise for
the sake of warmth, instead sludging, steadfast,
like an Armani foot soldier through road salt,
snowdrifts, and sleet, saying, "Some things
will not be compromised!"

Your method of slowly moving, methodically
passing through the house ... dusting, resetting
souvenirs, just so. You, the feng shui master
of knickknacks and fashion magazines, creating
a perfect order in the universe of our life.

Exit Strategy

Elaine took me to her German psychic;
as expected, she saw *everything*.

Our bad days and our glories.
The history of our times and species;
                   we have been together
                             for generations.

Realizing how long I have been with Elaine
made me feel tired — I didn't realize we'd been
working things out for over 400 years.
That's a long time to accommodate a sentient being,
I don't care what form I was in; me as:
           Her cat
           Her dog
           Her sister
           Her butler
           Her mother
           Her hairstylist,
Gerta saw it all against her inner astral cineplex.

I didn't know I was once a charming pistol-packing pescalero,
a handsome Mexican bandit who charmed Elaine
           (*in an earlier, even-more-succulent form*)
                       to indulge my desires.

Irresistible under a vast pecan tree.
The Milky Way strung over our heads.
I pick the flower she willingly offers me.
We melt into the warm night — two sentient beings
as happy as two souls could ever be.

She, the sheriff's daughter:
>> virgin, sixteen, flawless,
>>> filled with secret flames.

Me, hanging from a pecan tree:
>> limp, twitching, forlorn,
>>> looking a bit bewildered.

Too many lives to hold in one small boat.
Yet on we sail, east to Paradise,
>> fighting our way toward enlightenment,
>> the only exit strategy
>>> for two weary souls.

13

Hearing Perfectly

"You're missing all the high-pitched, soft-consonant
sounds," the audiologist told me.
"You mean women's voices?"
"Well, yes, I guess you could say that."

Isn't it odd, how men suffer this deafness?

We stare intently with sympathetic smiles, watching
their lips shower us in sentences half heard.

I've noticed that missing so much of what she tells me
has deepened my affection for her.

Is this what they mean by making more out of less?

How to Land a Man

Beauty, intelligence, and wit
are the insecticide of mosquito
men.

Who eat their dinners over the sink,
coveting their:
>Old shoes
>Worn shirts
>Endless routines
>Knowing it all.

Beauty must wander this
lumberyard of slumbering interest
in soft moccasins.

And in perfect harmony to his buzzing
hum:
>You're so dear
>You're so brave
>You're my exceptional man.

Feeding him a two-course meal of:
>1. Beauty
>2. Adoration.

She learns precision as she becomes
the architect of romance.
Rising perfectly each night,
>evaporating with the sun,
>>in her costume
>>>of indifference.

Redhead

I have a girl friend; she's 40 years older than I.
We say it's unfair to have met when age and polio
have left her youthfulness behind. When I am with
her, being is like breathing and long silences are as
productive as two-hour conversations. Love often
finds us this way —

> *Right person, wrong place*
> *Wrong time, right person*
> *Right woman, near death.*

She told me that when I am 75, I'll realize how everything
only gets worse. When the ones you love die, new ones no
longer take their place. But I tell her she's wrong.

Life dealt us its cruel card. We won't be jumping into
flaming beds with the passion of young bodies. Rather,
I will roll her wheelchair or lift her off the ground when
she topples over. I will be happy to hold her in my heart
as a perfect moment when love blew through the right
window at the wrong time.

You Never Left

After you died, I kept you near.
I brought you with me to parties.
I placed you in the trunk of my car,
close to my CD changer and the
music we loved — together.

I felt cheated to be left with only
memories of you. You filled so much
space. A nature so luminous it lit the
dark river path we walked along that
autumn before you left me — alone.

So I'll keep you and set you on the
table during poker night, or next to my
pillow as I sleep, or amidst the floral
arrangement at the museum ball.

"You look lovely in brass and silver
tonight. Is your lid screwed on tight?
Would you mind if I shake you, baby,
pop your top and sprinkle you on my
Caesar salad?"

"Just look at them looking. They're all green
with envy. I'm with the prize. One whose
beauty they all wish they could possess."

I think I will keep you with me forever.

Los Huesos
(the bones)

I sit with the dead tonight. I have
brought my father's tobacco and
my grandfather's beer. Between
their tombstones, I light a sparkler
and (*with eyes open*) imagine them
standing and dancing before me.
So I get up and dance with them,
turning, spinning, and falling to the
ground. As I catch my breath, I look
up to see their smiles shine down
like porcelain stars. They point at me.
"There's our boy; he's come to
drink and smoke with us. He loves
the lost ones with a heart as big as
heaven and inhales our graves as if
they were fields of red roses."

The beer widens my eyes, makes
the deep night opaque, revealing
a tribe of dead lovers who protect
us from devils and demons, insuring
our first communions and last rites,
ready to welcome us back home
with cold, soft hands.

The graveyard is full. The living
and their dearly departed sit in tight
family circles telling old stories that
recall ancestors whose names have
now been given to babies.

We pass funeral cards, rosaries, and
wedding rings among us — tiny monuments
to people whose portraits hang along the
stairs leading to the cellar where we make
our candles, crush hot peppers, and shed
our tears.

We slice lemon cake, eat chicken breasts,
and drink tequila in the Cementerio de Santa
Rosa. The ghosts are all brown, except mine.
Pale faces who've passed over — German,
pot-bellied, serious white people, who,
in life, had things to accomplish.

We sing and dance to all the dead gone.
Mock death and remember a cast of bit
players who slip into our dreams with
whispers just before dawn.

As I pour my tequila into the earth, I see
their spirit mouths open and skeletons
rise to dance three feet above the ground.
White vapor swirling like clouds. Sweet
misty blankets that embrace the tombs
of my family.

This Is Your Dream

As terrorists drag you out of our bedroom, I shout from the warmth of quilt and covers, "I should have married you!" and, "I was wrong about everything."

Shocked and realizing your death is imminent, you respond, "I think your new haircut looks swell, makes you look a lot younger," and, "Thanks for taking me to Mexico last summer — you're so dear."

With black stockings pulled over their faces, we see only their pale, cold, blue eyes. They speak a foreign language of neo-conservatism and politely wait for us to finish our final words before taking you outside to shoot you on our perfectly landscaped front lawn.

When you wake, you are glad to have me spooned beside you. Your usual annoyance at my snoring has turned to gratitude — affection, really. You kiss me awake and tell me how grateful you are to have a liberal boyfriend like me.

Suppressed anger is often the target of nocturnal insurgencies.

Saks Fifth Avenue

Time moves so slowly as we wait for
our loved ones to exit the dressing room
— again.

Exotic birds parade before us:
Tight-fitting
      Low-riding
           Up-lifting
                Miracle bras
moving in synchronous motion
          from rack to stack.

My male comrades and I
          warm the bench.
We're the second stringers.
Shoes
      Accessories
          Lingerie
            Lipstick
              Eye shadow.
You exit a new woman.

Almost Patrick

15ᵗʰ / Ides of March

Sick with the flu; and a good day to celebrate the
treachery of politicians. Elaine told me, "You
needed to get sick." *(What does she mean by
that?)*

Had soup with dry toast; went to bed early.

16ᵗʰ / My Birthday

Slept late, and woke feeling better. Skipped the
gym. Got a haircut.

Elaine sent me a provocative birthday card *(She
knows how stuff like that gets me going.)*. She
said, "You've got lots of testosterone for a guy
your age; who cares if you're losing your hearing?
You're usually more worried about sex than
listening anyway."

Bought a pizza, watched March Madness, had a
beer. Never thought turning 55 would be this
nice.

Drove past a bunch of drunks at 8:00 a.m. on
Water Street. "It's an American Drinking
Holiday," I tell my daughter. We drive around
talking about bands and listening to music. She's
17, wise, and tells me, "You still look a lot
younger than 55; who cares if you're shrinking
and your ears appear to be growing?"

I'd be Patrick if my mom had waited fifteen
minutes to give birth, but I guess some of us just
aren't born lucky.

My Youth

Dating that crazed, heartbreaking Italian,
wanting to die as my first feelings bleed all over
the sidewalk;

        W. B. Yeats in my backpack,
                true love, my religion.

Youth is painful.

Pretending the zit on my nose wasn't as big as a condo,
and that, at sixteen, such things didn't really matter.
        Are you looking in my eyes or at my pimple?

I now understood how women with large breasts must feel.

The schizophrenia of wanting to be unique and yet fit in.
Wanting to be liked, but hating what you had to do for it.

Youth is confusion.

The irreconcilable newsflash from my mother that,
"You're not so special!"
She, protecting me from Vanity Falls.

Failing in the laboratory of French kissing.
Thinking how it is an acquired taste like beer.
Her mouth awash with the scent of garlic —
a remnant of the Italian restaurant and the dinner
I bought, hoping to warm her toward the submarine races.

First Blood

"Your daughter's started her period!"
"What should I do?"
"Nothing, you're the dad.
Dads aren't supposed to know."

10 + ½ years is too soon.
She'll figure it all out.
Get it on with tampons, maxi pads, and Midol.
Doesn't seem fair. Showing up so early
when she still wants to be a boy.
Runs faster than any boy.

Of course, I don't know about it.
Not invited into the Women-Only Blood Club.
Staying clueless — the elegantly simpler gender.

My mind works on an impromptu ol'-dad-soft-shoe:
      circle of women, full moon,
      the ebb and the flow,
      women's secrets, sisterhood,
      and the Goddess Girls' Club,
but it's not working.
Nothing sacred about any of this for me.

When I get home, I hug her:
"Let's go for a Coke and a hamburger"
      … as if nothing's happened.
Just your same old dad. The old, safe shoe.
Feeling sad for she who must now bleed in secret, alone.

She Sees the Stars

Elaine was giddy. "I'm in Heaven!" she squeaked.

"That's why I brought you to LA, honey buns," I demurred.

She didn't know of my past life around people named: Keitel, Foster, Hopper, Costner, Arkin, Penn, Tarantino, and Travolta. What's the big deal? They wear pants with zippers, tie their shoes, have two ears — just like I.

But I was working hard to exceed her expectations. I admit, I'd fallen short a few times. But at middle age, I had learned the value of turning off the TV and giving my girl some fun — *her* kind of fun.

I sipped the champagne and held her purse. "I've never seen so many celebrities," she said, snapping pictures.

"Hey, babe, there's Faye Dunaway," or, "Oh, there's Robert Downey, Jr." I spotted stars like they were new lunar constellations waltzing down the runway, bellying up to the bar, all in a sea of lipstick and air kisses.

Elaine was ravenous. A celebrity cannibal. "I can't believe I am here. Oh my god, you're so cute."

Her frenzy lasted six hours; and even after she fell asleep, she was still smiling. She was drunk with happiness *(and she doesn't drink)*.

Me? I hate awards dinners, I hate wearing a jacket and tie, I hate air travel, and I tolerate champagne. But that day, Elaine knew I did it all for *her*.

Right Foot into Wings

My worst curse — immobility.
Crutches and no car for six weeks.
The basement writing room has
become a sensory-deprivation chamber.

Even my pain medication haunts me —
midgets in white doctors' jackets chasing
me with whips, offering me more pills.

All I can do is — hop, hop, hop.

"You needed this," Elaine tells me.
"A divine light will appear, a voice in
the night, an angel will come; you'll be
forever changed. You want to change,
don't you? You could use a little changing,
you know. Think transubstantiation's easy?
Huh? Do you? How about making the move
from caterpillar to butterfly? Think that's
so easy? Stop complaining and be glad
you have one good foot."

No pity down here in the deprivation chamber.
            Shut up, and take it like a man.
                        Life's a trash can — deal with it.

Alone in the basement — hop, hop, hop.
Entertaining pain-medication dwarfs — hop, hop, hop.
Writing fiction only a fleeting idea — hop, hop, hop.

Six weeks until transubstantiation liftoff.
            Fly to Mexico amidst clouds of Monarchs.
                        Butterfly wings better than any right foot.

My Cat's Human

I would tell my daughters, "That's the luckiest cat in the world; she's so dumb, she'd die if she ever stepped foot out the door."

I guess even she knew that; the day I left the front door open by mistake, freedom beckoned as she stared out into the wild world, knowing it wasn't for her.

I didn't pet her; she didn't like to be petted. I freshened her water. My daughters were always too busy to do it. She was my daughters' cat.

No one brushed her dreadlocks: the matted clumps that grew worse as she aged, slowed down, and slept more. So I did.

I grew up on a mink farm. I don't love animals. What are they good for, except to eat and wear?

She'd sit next to my desk as I'd write and stare and talk to no one. She'd sleep outside my bedroom waiting for me to wake up, scratching the door if I was late.

She didn't get smarter with time. After thirteen years, she was still just a dumb cat. Well, animals are all pretty dumb, aren't they?

Yesterday, she didn't get up from the place where she'd plant herself until I got home — the spot at the top of the steps where she seemed to be glued as if she were waiting for someone to come in the front door.

When I called Elaine to say the vet had just put Princess down, I made a joke about her corny name and started to weep. That was when I realized she'd made me her human.

Our Four-Year Anniversary

My girl friend and I have broken up
five times in four years: she = 3   me = 2
(*Although she says I'm responsible for all five*).
We often flip roles playing the perpetrator and
the deeply confused.

These vacations from our relationship showed
us how exhausting relating can really be.
Making the infrequent static of our daily union
seem like perfection. Sometimes distance does
make the heart grow fonder, and from those distances
we'd spin back to our predictable, comfortable center.

We now think this history is the heart and soul
of our connection. It is the holy litany of time spent,
battles compromised, relentless measuring,
assessing, the distrusting and trusting of feelings.

Our fertilizer was not the temptation of pheromones,
high heels, blood-red lips, tight jeans, or calypso music
amidst clouds of Camel Straights, but a forced march
over an undulating landscape called our history.

Schnook

I should have ended it two years ago.
But I'm lazy. A lover of predictable
routine.

You wanted us to live together.
I wanted one night a week.

You wanted me to be present
and bend to your needs.

I wanted to remain true to my
lazy nature.

I guess that makes me opportunistic.
The kind of guy women talk about
when they recite the ways in which a
dog is better than a boyfriend.

Sometimes I think only another man
could see what divinity doth lurk in
the heart of a schnook.

But still I should have known.
I should have ended the fantasy
that you and I would live happily
ever after — sooner.

Kiss a frog, get a prince in pond water.

Below the Floor

I live in the basement
beneath the footsteps.
The furnace whistles to me on cold days.
The washing machine hums to me at night.

My ex-wife lives one floor above,
10,000 miles away.
My daughters, with wings,
sail between heaven and earth,
getting honey from the clouds
and iron from the brown soil.

My possessions are ideas.
My lovers' names all rhyme.
My conquests are fictionalized.

The shadow side of home sweet home,
where a giant prowls naked
beneath the floor, and ideas
grow during intercourse.

Influences of Light

It happens each early summer.
She backs off her anti-depressants,
thinking more UV rays can substitute
for her drugs. She comes out swinging,
determined to reclaim what is
rightfully hers.

For a day or a week, she's a warrior
but quickly fades into a humble,
tumble, pile of bewilderment. (It's
hard to sustain determination on
just sunlight. Warmth alone isn't
enough to help you think straight.)

Following her short freedom flight,
she becomes earthbound, a cloud
that hovers low against a county trunk
road — a vaporous curtain that flattens
and abducts you.

But you drive on, and eventually pass
through it, through her. And bring her to
a small hill where you ask her to look
a great distance and remember tomorrow
or yesterday or her true nature with the ease
of her winter-fresh mind.

The Last Time

I was thinking about the last time
I was in love. When I realized she
was thinking the same things at the
same time I was. The constant
erection, forgetfulness, and tears.
Everywhere was a bed. Every day our
hearts bled into buckets big enough
to wet the thirst of 1,000 red roses.

Do you suppose love — true love — parts
the curtain and allows angels and night visitors
to circle this light? A light that smells like cinnamon
and sounds like children's whispers.
We had only to breathe the same air to believe it.

Seven months later, she returned to her husband and
the sad chains. Love hasn't shown up since, except
when I find her in the features of people I see.
This nose, those eyes, that chin. They remind me of
the last time I was in love.

In This Movement of Air

We stand in twilight,
knowing meaning will
come as it always does.

Some things are beyond our
control:

> The migration of birds
> The end of love
> The Harvest Moon
> The inevitability of war.

This ebb and our flow are as
fixed and predictable as the
certainties of gravity.

Raising our eyes toward the night
sky, we embrace beneath a rain
of falling leaves, and celebrate
the autumn of our time here.

Anti–Gravity Man

He tried to fill the hole — find
the center of what fell out of him
fifteen minutes before midnight
on the day he was born.

It was his benign tumor. A sickness
that wouldn't kill him. At night,
before sleep entered his room,
before twilight clouds brushed
his eyes closed, he'd reach
inside and wonder why he was
made this way. A mutation with an
unnatural lightness of being.

His condition went undetected, except
when the wind blew through him,
causing his shirt to billow like a sail,
and a high-pitched whistle to emit from
within him. A sound only a dog's ears
could detect.

To himself, he was invisible:
tissue-paper thin, weightless, and
lacking substance. Most days, he
felt he wasn't even standing on
earth. But he wanted to.

He theorized that a heart must hold the
universe and weigh ten thousand
pounds. It is a heart that keeps
feet on the floor.

Nothing mattered to this untethered,
floating pilgrim but finding a cure
for his gaping hole. A yearning he
did not acknowledge until the day
he became firmly rooted in her.

Miss Valley City, North Dakota

It was an odd place to be a beauty queen,
butt square in the middle of America.
Where drinking, eating red meat,
and killing time outside Woolworth's
was considered gainful employment.

A Great Plains beauty with a lost look
from a past life that told you she
wasn't comfortable wearing this town's
tiara. Wondering why any thinking God
would re-enter her *here*. In this place,
to eat buffalo burgers and to be confused
with someone else. Making amends for
past life sins.

Maybe this is why she tried to drink her
brains out. Pounding away her sense of
strangeness to make her soul fit here, but
drunk or not, they loved her and voted
her their Queen of Valley Days in 1972.

They wrapped their beauty queen's
head in a garland of Prairie Chicken
grass, gave her a scepter of wheat
husks, circled her ivory porcelain
neck with a string of Swedish meatballs,
and carried her down Main Street in a
white Chevy convertible chariot.

Years later, after she dried out, moved
away, began to live in real time and
remember her days, she made friends
with life and walked the middle road
between drunks and born-again Christians.
She discovered she could zap pain
away with a flick of her forefinger.
She liked doing this better than
drinking and began to live dangerously.

In time, she yearned to return to
that white convertible and smell
it all over again. To see it with
young, sober eyes at middle age.
The people outside Woolworth's
were glad to see her. Pleased to
have her flick her finger their way.
She would always be Miss Valley
City. And she came to know that
family is family, and the glue that
binds us together is greater than
the things that make us change.

Feathers for Carlos

I went to my first singles mixer last night. Or rather,
I entered the room that overlooked the patio, where
singles fluttered about like feathers from one shoulder
to the other.

It was a snowstorm of feathers, rising, falling, landing,
leaning, seeking a soft, safe place to rest. As I looked
out over that patio of desires, where hearts emit silent but
detectable love calls, I felt myself reconsider whether
I want to join this sea of seekers. Maybe my heart is
whole and not in need of one true love or her expectant
arms of warm saltwater.

Arms in which to float and wander — bobbing gently —
up and down, and up and down — as I gaze into
an August sky on a day so humid the rain falls like mist.

I considered all this as I stood there looking, wondering
whether I should step into that yearning river. And I
turned and decided to go home.

It was just cowardice on my part. I told myself I'll
return another day to seek out the most listless of these
feathers. I'll then hold her in my fingertips and ask her
to marry me, and we'll live happily ever after in the
pink hollow of my soft, warm hands.

North American Love Poem

Why else would Latin blood flow through the veins of two cold Eastern Europeans?

How else could we melt the snow or vaporize the rain that fell around us?

Groves of palm trees sprang up out of our very footsteps. We were the Tropic of Cancer walking down NP Avenue in Fargo, North Dakota, in the dead of winter. Beneath our snowmobile suits, earmuffs, and insulated boots, we were two tropical birds who, when rubbed together, create sumptuous coconut oil.

God made no mistake when He let Elaine have her way with me that night in January at early dusk. I expected premeditated pain. I expected nothing but the end. I'd long since given up on the rumor that women — the right woman — led men like me to our subterranean souls.

But she made the middle ground a spacious place. She saw the possibilities of quiet diligence, erotic surprise, and sweet kindness, pouring love in doses so incremental it fooled me into thinking love was not burning a hole in me.

Sex for Liver

It was the cosmic glue of our love. The outward
expression of my inability to be romantic. We
transcended irritation, bad weather, and snowstorms
locked securely in our love capsule.
Until the day her anti-depressant kicked in.
Until the day a posse of post-depression Greek
sex bandits named Lexapro, Paxil, Prozac, and
Zoloft rode down the middle of our bed and blew
up our love nest.

Seeking the balance that medication brought her,
but wanting the pleasures of intimacy, she searched
for the right pharmaceutical drug. Promising sex,
with only the side effect of liver damage or death
(only one of every 250,000 actually *die*), she came
upon Serzone.

"Yes, but what if it kills you? Or ruins your liver?"
Maybe my desires, my passions would kill her?

She'd already given up drugs (at least the illegal ones)
and alcohol, too. She had surrendered her anxiety
disorder and depression to popular medication, but
chanted, "God damn it, I'm not giving up sex!"

I loved her perverse sense of justice. It wasn't based
on logic, but rather on passion. "Well, as long as it's
going to wreck your liver, why not just start drinking
again?"

"No, I'm staying sober." Again, her perverse logic.
The unpredictable universe between her ears.
The broadest canvas a writer could hope to find.
She was better than my fiction. I awed at the vistas
I saw in her. The river of tears that coursed through
her sleepless, sexless nights as she clung to a life that
had gone ipso-flipso.

She knew what she was willing to sacrifice.
We knew what we had to do, and that night,
had liver and onions before going to bed early
in order to get a few extra rounds in. It seemed
like the only holistic, symbolic, metaphoric thing
to do.

Dear Clara

I am sorry I haven't communicated much lately.
Like many men, I am of few words. Dull, really. I've
been seeing that "hoochie mama" I told you about last
summer. She has turned out to be very fine — calm and
spacious.

She is not perfect. She has her monkeys, too.
Depression, alcoholism, and an endless search
for the answers. But her pan-fried fishballs,
stillness, and sexual appetite leave me satisfied.

When I am with her, I can breathe. She is content with
my once-a-week visits. We're like strangers crossing the
desert, who rest for a moment under the shadow of a palm
tree. We share shade in common. Shade is enough for me
now.

So starting over with you is out of the question. Daunting.
Exhausting me before I even set one foot out the door.
You see, I have discovered the miracle of the desert's
silence, where secrets of the heart lie beneath hot, shifting
sands.

South for a Season

A few weeks ago, a friend of mine
had a nervous breakdown. Break through?
Too many volts running through a
six-amp spinal cord. A mind bursting
with people and ideas that were not meant to
be there. Or maybe, it's the normal mind
free of work, obligation, and traffic
laws. The ol' Alice Through the Looking
Glass, king has no clothes, nothing
looks as it appears dilemma.
Maybe she didn't have a breakdown
at all, but was suspended by a thread
of sanity above an ocean of chaos,
and she just needed to jump.

I don't know.

When I saw her, she wept in sorrow.
Her tongue was heavy with anti-anxiety,
anti-depressant, anti-psychotic drugs she
calls her Vitamin Z. She sounded like I do
on too many beers, but without my
cheery, drunken disposition. "I want to
kill myself. I am sick of being a weirdo-
cripple-psycho-handicapper," she moaned.

She had worked harder at self improvement than
anyone I know. Doing all the right things: yoga,
massage, holistic diet, tribal drumming, and a
daily litany of positive affirmations. She was
thoughtful and fearful that her craziness would
return like a migratory flock of insanity
and steal her mind for another season.

What It Isn't

I used to think that love was
the electrical charge that passed
between the groins of strangers
searching for perfect union.

Later, I thought love, mature love,
was recognizing the abundance
of space that circled one certain
someone. And drowning in this
tranquil pond of silence and rest.

Still later, after my first divorce,
I lowered my expectations, as
experience and life tend to make
us do, and felt friendship was love's
seed. If nurtured, it would ignite
into passionate flames — maybe.

After my second divorce, I
wondered if it was only the brief
predictable space between two lips,
two half-opened eyelids. Just before
day disrupts the clarity of the groggy.

Now, I realize how illusory
and without definition love is.
Transparent, weightless, out
of time, unattainable. A sun
that rises only to burn hope
from hearts exhausted in
the act of anticipation.

End Zone

10 a.m. Sunday mass is long since
past. The congregation says, "Amen,"
and the pitcher is passed. The seven-
point mystery of the NFL begins.
A bleeding stigmata of crimson and
red on 100 yards of green pig skin.
65,000 paid guests drinking,
screaming, talking about point
spreads.

I see holy ghosts in the end zone.
Wolverines braying at the Warren Moon.

Time stops. The ball hangs suspended
above the goal post. This moment.
Your smile. The sweet smell of beer
on your breath. The cold, damp redness
of your nose. The hoarse whisper
of your voice — signs to me that God
is near and the outcome of a life is as
unpredictable as a Hail Mary pass.

Fly, Fall, Dreaming

Sometimes when my mind wanders, it feels like I am walking down a steep city street almost falling, as if I am flying and dreaming. In my dream, a great wave cascades over my bald spot, as if it were an island in a sky-blue Mediterranean sea. Maybe dreams are like flying, falling.

I sit in the town square across from The Parroquia, the great cathedral in San Miguel de Allende. It rises pink and brown in the early morning light. A woman dressed in white with a blood-red shawl enters, making signs of the cross so quickly that I think she is swatting at flies or some invisible demon, but this is just her private ritual as she enters church. This is her crazy way of falling or dreaming. The arrangement we make in our minds with no one but ourselves.

I love the faces of the Indians. They are darker, more bronze in color than Spaniards. A young Indian girl walks toward me with the sun on her face. It is as if she is wearing a mask of polished copper. Her skin is radiant in the morning light, as she quickly passes by without looking at me. What is her dream? Does she yearn to fall, too? Are we alike in this way?

San Miguel de Allende is a city built in the clouds on the shoulders of nine churches. The buildings are painted yellow, orange, red, green, and white, like great tropical birds. They stand against a clear, blue sky. It is easy to fall here. Time moves so slowly on this mountain of silver and dreaming.

Two broad-bottomed housemaids walk by, wearing uniforms the color of orange sherbet. They carry a large, green garbage container between them as they pass me in the early morning mist on their way to work. They are dreaming, too. I can tell because their eyelids are closed, but their eyes are moving.

At dawn, people pour buckets of water onto the cobblestone sidewalks outside their homes and shops. Sweeping them with brooms that look like witches' riding sticks, they wash yesterday's debris away, yesterday's fallen dreams into the gutter. Sidewalks must be clean to carry dreamers.

Me? What is my dream? In Mexico, I become Latin and romantic. Maybe looking at these women whose faces glisten like copper in the morning light makes me feel this way. Or perhaps it is the thin mountain air that gives my dreams room to rise up and find me. My dream today is for a lover. My dream doesn't require her to grow old with me and rub my forehead as I lie dying. She only needs to fill my dream time. My moment here and now.

Isn't that why we dream? To have the impossible for just a moment? To reach for things beyond our grasp during those times when falling and dreaming live suspended above our kitchen sink, answering machine, and dinner table?

Sad Visitor

She'd come sometimes
at the oddest moments.
Popping up out of nowhere.

Visiting last night in my dream,
she wore only a purple bra, garter, and stockings.
Even her small, triangular tuft
          of pubic hair was purple.

It always surprised me
when she appeared in just this way.

I ran my hand over the soft
          curve of her ass.
She touched my face, and I could
          see she was sad.
Sad to be visiting in this lost lover's shadow.

In a blink, I am carried to the street below
her downtown apartment.
We yearn for each other,
but she does not invite me in
          as we slowly evaporate into night mists,
                    sailing home to empty bodies.

Ghost Boy's Last Supper

Ghost boy stood cool, silent next to her lips,
"All my words have fallen into your brown eyes,
10,000 miles deep, and warm as tropical rain.
Even the breeze that blew through me has fallen into you."

Promising to turn my salt tears
to raindrops of diamonds.
Phoenix feathers to dust doom away.
Howling as I become her last supper.

Resurrected, I recover myself under shoeboxes,
dust balls, and lost socks.
Dancing like a lover liberated
under a summer-night sky,
turning as everything became
clear and brilliant and slow.

Waking to find myself between two pure porcelain legs,
inviting me in as if invitation were breathing
and passion were a soft, warm breeze
blowing across her breasts at 1:15 p.m. on Sunday.

Our Time Ending

It's broken now. Fallen to a floor
that does not care about possibilities.
Placed in a closet of lost things,
it's a testimony that our passion
had no privilege.

Nothing is in vain. We'll make this
the monument of our time together, as we
consider what became of our symmetry.

Birch Street

Sitting on the porch outside my walk-up with Elaine,
watching the Friday night action on Birch Street.
Southside's so humid the air weeps.

Elaine and I are weeping, too.
Silent tears of solidarity.
She's so full of Prozac she can't sleep, and
I'm so drunk I can't think straight.
Her depression and my beer free our tears
from the jail we carry in our hearts.

Neighbors and strangers pass by in the water vapor.
Walking in twos and fours. Driving by in suped-up
cars and wrecks. Skinny, greased-up gangbangers
with pants so big they sweep the street, and girlfriends
in dresses so tight they burn my eyes.

I can smell Miguel's Taco Stand. Hear the cool
Mexican music he plays. Sometimes I wish Elaine
were Mexican. Hot, sweet, and the ruler of my passion;
but she's from North Dakota, a silent state where
you drink to feel and dance and cry.

Sailing, drifting down Birch Street. Misty boats,
street shufflers, and señoritas. Off to their somewhere.
I contemplate how empty my can of beer is and
how long I can live with a woman who cries all day.

Mondays are better. I sober up and lay lines for the
gas company. Good, clean work. Work that gives me
time to think about moving to that little town in central
Mexico I visited twenty years ago, before Birch Street,
Elaine, and three kids nailed my ass to this porch.

In Retrospect

It is through the death or absence of things
that I find their value. I take them all for granted
until they are gone.

> Until the cat is dead
> Until my wife has left
> Until I stop wanting.

Is this how men discover their feelings?

I have begun to keep close watch on this
migration of absences and passings. The holes
created by my thinking precious is relative,
or hidden in a flock of distractions.

> Birth
> School
> Work
> Death

So what? Is any of it really so important?

I love more now, not because love has grown within
me, but because I have discovered *sorrow* when
that which has stood faithfully near is gone.

Thin Sip of Ice Water

She sat so straight, and
        she was so thin.
I began to wonder if perhaps she were made of cardboard.
Some kind of promotional stand-up for
        proper posture and diction.
Coiffeured with a Texas big-hair halo,
        patent-leather shoes, and pearl necklace.
She blazed with intellectual perfection.

While a slim slice of pizza, to be sure,
I still wanted a bite of her, but such erect,
schooled, well-turned-out women
can be long, cold roads to walk.
Yet I persisted, ignoring her enigmatic stare that
told me none of my pitches were in the strike zone.

And why was I even trying to warm this glacier?
I guess hoping hot lava ran beneath such cold-weather veins.
Sweet surrender and Patsy Cline might co-habit this vision
in black velvet.

As she rose to leave, I knew I'd failed —
        the Ice Age would continue.
Kissing me with the passion of an arctic bullfighter yelling
"Toro, Toro, Toro, el Bad Monk Bandito!" she took my
breath away and ran her toreador's sword through my heart.
Rose petals and blood drops fell to the floor as she walked
to the exit, dragging her red cape behind her.

I watched as a breeze lifted her thin frame
and carried her like lavender tissue into a morning pool
that lay beneath my bed where dreams wait to waken
        and die softly into sleep.

The Mystery of Waters

The Black River moved east to the Red Sea
as August crept in on soft hands,
all before a lost tribe of clowns
carrying cartoons and sacred images
high above their heads,
        close to the blue sky,
            close to their desires.

Calliope music beckoned them enter the
cathedral that nestled under a grand mustard tree,
as Mary Magdalene flew high above the center ring,
        Saint Agnes recited the seven truths,
           Lucifer blew fire and ice,
ending the world as predicted by Frost.

Alice, their queen, kept watch —
Alice, who knew the secret of grinning cats and wise
caterpillars smoking dope high above the cathedral on tree
limbs, purring to perfection in sitting meditation,
        dreaming of dancing mice,
           one-minded mischief makers.

I remained silent and floated on to the Dead Sea,
where blood drops become rosebuds in bleeding hearts.
Watching ash fall from the hand of an avatar,
        snowflakes in August
           dusting me white as talcum after baptism.

These wandering mysteries.
        These puzzlements of mind.
Meditations on the nature of rivers and seas,
breezes that dapple my mind in sunlight at midnight.

Will you float with me
on this river of grace?
Belly button pointing toward heaven,
umbilical eye staring into the mystery of love.

When Penis Walked the Earth
(Milwaukee Journal Sentinel; December 2, 2003)

I never thought of it as evolving. At least not like this.
Never thought about when it first raised its proud little
head.

But a 425-million-year-old fossil found in Herefordshire,
England, changed all that. The oldest record of an animal
that was inarguably male made me stop and take stock. A
tiny crustacean, only two-tenths of an inch long — with an
unmistakable penis.

They christened it *Colymbosathon Ecplecticos*, which
means "amazing swimmer with a large penis."

Scientists say it had copulatory organs one-third the length
of its body. Wow. Makes a guy sit back and think about
all the evolutionary outcomes. The cars we'd drive or the
clothes we'd wear.

Monkeys became men.
Fish learned to fly.
Penises roamed prehistoric Earth.
I guess some things never change.

Valentine

They're complex,
these things we
build our hearts around.

Charles P. Ries'

narrative poems, short stories, interviews, and poetry reviews have appeared in over two hundred print and electronic publications. He has received four Pushcart Prize nominations for his writing and is the author of six books of poetry. He was awarded the Wisconsin Regional Writers Association "Jade Ring" Award for humorous poetry and is the former poetry editor of *Word Riot* and *ESC!*. Charles is the author of The Fathers We Find, a somewhat-fictionalized memoir of his growing up on a mink farm in Southeastern Wisconsin. His work is archived in the Charles P. Ries Collection at Marquette University.

A citizen philosopher, Ries lived in London and North Africa after college, where he studied the mystical teachings of Islam known as Sufism. In 1989, he worked with the Dalai Lama on a program that brought American religious- and psycho-therapists together for a weeklong dialogue. He has done extensive work with men's groups and worked with a Jungian psychotherapist for over five years, during which time he learned to find meanings in small things.

Ries has begun work on a second novel, A Life by Invitation, which will follow his rise as a mystic in North Africa and his subsequent floundering while living in Los Angeles, all of which has convinced him of the time-honored wisdom: "Wherever you go, there you are," and, "This isn't Kansas, Dorothy."

Ries is also a founding member of the Lake Shore Surf Club, the oldest freshwater surfing club on the Great Lakes.

Acknowledgments

The author would like to thank the following print and electronic publications where the poems in this collection first appeared:

Free Verse, Clark Street Review, Barbaric Yawp, Zen Baby, Shoes, Arbor Vitae, Wisconsin Poets' Calendar, *Anthills,* Cinnamon Press, *Press,* Folded Word Press, *Starry Night Review, Gloom Cupboard,* Valentine Peace Project, *Dispatch Literary Review, Andwerve, Zygote in My Coffee, Main Channel Voices, Underground Window, Mastodon Dentist, Sein und Werden, Angel Head, Mannequin Envy, Muses Review, Right Hand Pointing, Blind Man's Rainbow, Silt Reader, Unlikely Stories,* The Time Garden, *ART:MAG, Turk Magazine, Latino Stuff Review, Ya'Sou Poetry, The Moon, Blow Back Magazine,* Tree House Productions, Staplegun Press, *Monkey Kettle, Real Eight View, Quill and Parchment,* Fullosia Press, Laura Hird.com, *Tamafyhr Mountain Poetry, Spare Change News, Private Line, Thunder Sandwich, FUCK,* Lummox Press, *remark., Poetic Inhalation, Sidereality,* Muses Apprentice Guild, *Poetry Patchwork, Liquid Muse Quarterly, California Quarterly, Word Riot, HazMat Review, Half Drunk Muse, Nerve Cowboy, Pig Iron Malt, Circle Magazine, Rattle, Wellspring Journal, Anthology, Poetry Motel, Poiesis,* WTSC Potsdam, WUWM Milwaukee, and KSER Seattle.

What you are holding is the First Edition printing of this collection.

Colophon

The cover font is set in Bank Gothic Medium. The ornamental design of the title pages is called Free Ribbons and was created by Intellecta Design; the ampersand of the title is set in Goudy Bookletter 1911. All poem and section titles are set in Fiolex Girls and all other text is set in OldStyle 1, the latter created by HPLHS Prop Fonts. The tiny hearts of the Advanced Praise, Contents, and Other Works sections are from the Loves Devine collection, created by Ms. DeVine. All shoe footer silhouettes are from the WC Fetish Bta and WC Fetishist Bta collections, created by WC Fonts, wcfonts.com. All women's figure footer silhouettes are from the Darrian's Sexy Silhouettes 1, 2, 3, 4, and the Sexy Silhouette Stencils collections, created by Darrian Lynx, ©1999, 2003 Darrian Lynx and California Cosmo; all rights reserved. All fonts were used with permission, and the publisher wishes to thank the font creators for their generosity in allowing legal use.

*P*ropaganda *P*ress

♥ ♥ ♥ ♥ ♥ ♥ ♥ ♥ ♥ ♥

All of these books (and more!) are available at Propaganda
Press' website: alternatingcurrentarts.blogspot.com.

alternatingcurrentarts.blogspot.com

Made in the USA
Columbia, SC
20 February 2018